Anthems
for Choirs
3

**for sopranos and altos
(three or more parts)**

Edited by
PHILIP LEDGER

Oxford University Press

Music Department Walton Street Oxford OX2 6DP

Anthems
for Choirs
3

Edited by
PHILIP LEDGER

Preface

The two volumes *Anthems for Choirs 2* and *3* form a comprehensive collection for soprano and alto voices ranging from the 13th century to the present day. They are suitable for cathedral, church, school, women's, girls', and boys' choirs. Volume 2 is devoted to unison and two-part anthems whilst volume 3 comprises anthems in three or more parts and a set of five introits. Four new anthems have been specially commissioned from David Lord, John Rutter, Robert Sherlaw Johnson, and Phyllis Tate. With the exception of Christmas (most choir libraries already contain music for this festival) all seasons of the Church's year are represented in the collection. There are 24 anthems in each book.

The keyboard realizations in volume 2 are editorial and may be played on the organ, harpsichord, or piano; some dynamics, tempo indications, introductions, and vocal ornamentation have been incorporated into the text. Further information about individual anthems is to be found in the Appendix to each volume. Unless otherwise stated, English translations are by the Rev. W. M. Atkins.

I am most grateful to David Chadd, Charles Cudworth, Julian Rushton, Allan Tonkin, and many other friends for their advice and assistance in the preparation of these books.

Philip Ledger

Anthems for Choirs 1 for mixed voices (edited by Francis Jackson) is on sale.

Index of Titles and Opening Lines

Where opening lines differ from titles the former are shown in italics.

Anthems suitable for unaccompanied singing are marked thus *

continued overleaf

Index of Composers and Arrangers

For sources and further information see Appendix, page 100.

Seasonal Index

1. INTROIT FOR LENT OR PASSIONTIDE

PHINEAS FLETCHER
(1582—1650)

ORLANDO GIBBONS
(1583—1625)
arranged by PHILIP LEDGER

2. INTROIT FOR ADVENT

PHILIPP NICOLAI
Tr. G. R. Woodward
(1848—1934)

Melody by (?) PHILIPP NICOLAI
(1556—1608)
arranged by PHILIP LEDGER

Words used by permission of Schott & Co. Ltd.

© Oxford University Press 1973

3. INTROIT FOR EASTER

G. R. WOODWARD
(1848–1934)

Melody from DAVID'S PSALMEN,
Amsterdam, 1685
arranged by PHILIP LEDGER

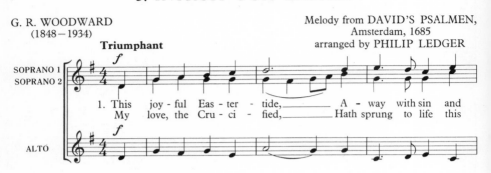

1. This joy - ful Eas - ter - tide,_____ A - way with sin and
My love, the Cru - ci - fied,_____ Hath sprung to life this

sor - - - row! Had Christ, that once was slain, ne'er burst his
mor - - - row.

Our faith had been in vain:
three - day pri - son, Our__ faith had been__ in__ vain: But

now hath Christ a - ris - en,__ a - ris - en, a -

Words used by permission of A. R. Mowbray & Co. Ltd.

- ris - en, a - ris - - - - - en.

Optional Refrain for v. 3

Unis.

Had Christ, that once was slain, ne'er burst his three-day pri - son, Our

Had Christ, that once was slain, ne'er burst his three-day pri - son, Our

mp cresc.

faith had been in vain: But now hath Christ a - ris - en,— a -

mp cresc.

faith had been in vain: But now hath Christ a - ris - en, a -

- ris - en, a - ris - en, a - ris - - - - en.

- ris - en, a - ris - en, a - ris - - - - en.

2. My flesh in hope shall rest
   And for a season slumber:
   Till trump from east to west
   Shall wake the dead in number.
   Had Christ, that once, etc.

3. Death's flood hath lost his chill,
   Since Jesus cross'd the river:
   Lover of souls, from ill
   My passing soul deliver.
   Had Christ, that once, etc.

4. INTROIT FOR ASCENSION

A. T. RUSSELL
(1806—1874)

Melody, *Ach, Herr, du allerhöchstes Gott*, Anon.
arranged by PHILIP LEDGER

2. The heav'ns with joy receive their Lord,
   By saints by angel-hosts adored;
   O day of exultation!
   Glad earth, adore thy mighty King;
   His rising, his ascension sing
   With thankful adoration.

3. Our great High Priest hath gone before,
   Now on his Church his grace to pour,
   And still his love he giveth:
   O may our hearts to him ascend,
   And all within us upward tend
   To him who ever liveth.

5. INTROIT FOR WHITSUN

PAUL GERHARDT (1607—1676)
Tr. G. R. Woodward
(1848—1934)

Melody by LOUIS BOURGEOIS
(1551)
arranged by PHILIP LEDGER

6. ALLELUIA PSALLAT

ANON.
13th Century

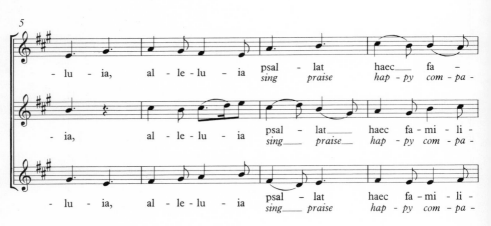

29

al - le -lu - ia psal - lat___ de - o lau - dum et pre - co - ni -
al - le -lu - ia sing praise to___ the___ Lord your God on

al - le -lu - ia psal - lat___ de - o lau - dum et pre - co - ni -
al - le -lu - ia sing___ praise to the Lord your God___ on___

al - le -lu - ia psal - lat___ de - o lau - dum et___ pre - co - ni -
al - le -lu - ia sing___ praise_ to the Lord your God___ on___

33

- a, et pre - co - ni - a } al - le - lu - ia,___
high, to the Lord your God on high }

- a, et___ pre - co - ni - a } al - le - lu - ia,
high, your___ God___ on high }

- a, et pre - co - ni - a } al - le - lu -
high, your___ God on high }

38

al - le - lu - ia,___ al - le -lu - ia, al - le -lu - ia,
al - le - lu - ia, al - le -lu - ia, al - le -lu - ia,
- ia, al - le - lu - ia, al - le -

43

al - le -lu - ia,___ al - le -lu - ia, al -le -lu - ia.
al - le - lu - ia, al - le - lu - ia.
- lu - ia, al - le - lu - ia.

7. QUAM PULCRA ES

JOHN of DUNSTABLE
(d. 1453)

8. O VOS OMNES

Lamentations I, v. 12

TOMÁS LUIS DE VICTORIA
(c. 1535–1611)

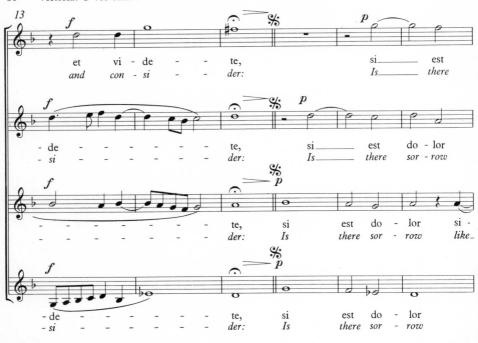

9. AVE REGINA CAELORUM

GUILLAUME DUFAY
(c. 1400 – 1474)

Con moto

SOPRANO

A - - - - ve re - gi - na cae - lo - - -
Hail_____ thee, queen on high in hea - - -

ALTO 1

A - - - ve re - gi - na cae - lo - -
Hail_____ thee, queen on high in hea - -

ALTO 2

A - - - ve re - gi - na cae - lo - - -
Hail_____ thee, queen on high in hea - - -

- rum, A - ve do - mi - na__ an - ge - lo - rum, Sal - -
- ven, Hail thee, ru - ler of__ an - ge - lic hosts, Hail

- rum, A - ve do - mi - na__ an - ge - lo - rum, Sal - -
- ven, Hail thee, ru - ler of__ an - ge - lic hosts, Hail

- rum, A - ve do - mi - na an - ge - lo - rum, Sal - -
- ven, Hail thee, ru - ler of an - ge - lic hosts, Hail

cresc.

- ve ra - dix sanc - ta, Ex qua mun - do lux est or - ta.
Mo - ther ho - ly, From whom on earth has ri - sen light.

cresc.

- ve ra - dix sanc - ta, Ex qua mun - do lux est or - ta.
Mo - ther ho - ly, From whom on earth has ri - sen light.

cresc.

- ve ra - dix sanc - ta, Ex qua mun - do lux est or - ta.
Mo - ther ho - ly, From whom on earth has ri - sen light.

10. O CRUX BENEDICTA

CLAUDIO MONTEVERDI
(1567—1643)

11. O DOMINE JESU CHRISTE

CLAUDIO MONTEVERDI
(1567 – 1643)

12. SURGENS JESUS

CLAUDIO MONTEVERDI
(1567 – 1643)

13. TWO CANONS

W. A. MOZART
(1756—1791)

a) ALLELUJA K.553

b) AVE MARIA K.554

14. IM HIMMELREICH EIN HAUS STEHT

(In Heaven doth a House rise)

WILL VESPER
Tr. Mrs. Bertram Shapleigh

MAX REGER
(1873—1916)

15. IN PRAISE OF GOD

Tr. Percy Pinkerton

FRANÇOIS COUPERIN
(1688–1733)
arranged by HECTOR BERLIOZ

Con - sa - crons_ nos airs_ Et nos_ con - certs, Con - sa -
Let_ us chant,_ in glad_ and true_ ac - cord, Songs of

Con - sa - crons, con - sa - crons_ nos airs_ Et nos con -
Let_ us chant, all in glad_ ac - cord,_ Our songs of

16. VENI, CREATOR

HECTOR BERLIOZ
(1803 – 1869)

According to Berlioz'directions, this motet may be accompanied by the organ, provided that the player confines himself to doubling the vocal parts in the same octave.

Ⓒ Oxford University Press 1973 (English text)

17. HYMN TO THE VIRGIN

DANTE
Tr. J. Troutbeck

GIUSEPPE VERDI
(1813—1901)

72
cresc.
ff
- ta - te, in te mag - ni - fi - cen - za, in te s'ad -
pi - ty, In thee ma - jes - tic great - ness, in thee u -
- ta - te, in te mag - ni - fi - cen - za, in te s'ad - u -
pi - ty, In thee ma - jes - tic great - ness, in thee u - nit -
- ta - te, in te mag - ni - fi - cen - za, in te s'ad - u - na
pi - ty, In thee ma - jes - tic great - ness, in thee u - nit - ed
- ta - te, in te mag - ni - fi - cen - za, in te s'ad - u - na
pi - ty, In thee ma - jes - tic great - ness, in thee u - nit - ed
76
p
pp
- u - na quan - tun - que in cre - a - tur - a è di bon -
- nit - ed What - e'er of good - ness dwells in a - ny
- na quan - tun - que in cre - a - tur - a è di bon -
- ed What - e'er of good - ness dwells in a - ny
quan - tun - que in cre - a - tur - a è di bon -
What - e'er of good - ness dwells in a - ny
quan - tun - que in cre - a - tur - a è di bon -
What - e'er of good - ness dwells in a - ny
81
allarg.
più p
ancora più p
- ta - te. A - ve! A - ve!
crea - ture. All hail! All hail!

18. O BONE JESU

JOHANNES BRAHMS
(1833—1897)

No. 1 of *Drei geistliche Chöre*, Opus 37 (1866)

19. PSALM 13
(Opus 27)

Tr. Sally Wright

JOHANNES BRAHMS
(1833–1897)

20. PSALM 150

(Based on an old French melody)

Melody, with words by Théodore de Bèze,
from the French Psalter of 1562
★English translation: 1632

ZOLTÁN KODÁLY
(1882—1967)

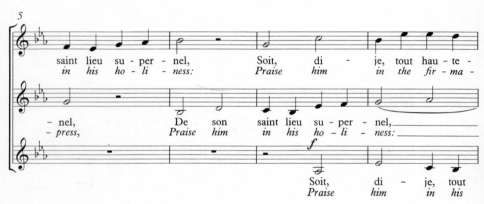

★English text chosen by Ruth Douglass

This anthem is published separately (W72).

© Oxford University Press 1966

21. SONG OF THE SUN

St. Francis of Assisi

CARL ORFF

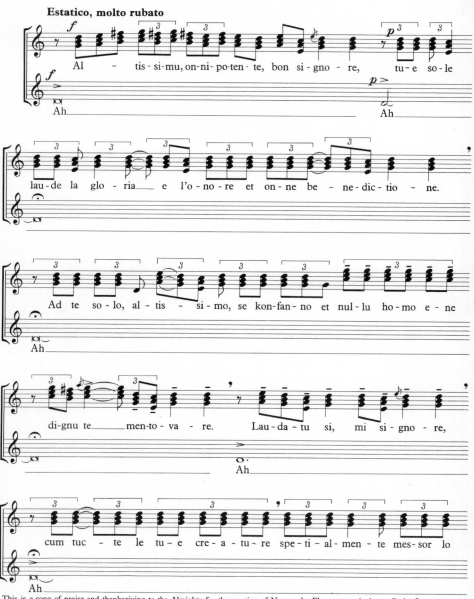

This is a song of praise and thanksgiving to the Almighty for the creation of Nature, the Elements, and, above all, the Sun.

fra - te so - le,___ lo qua - le lo ior - no al - lu - me - ni   per   nui;   et

el - lu è bel - lu e ra - di - an - te cum gran - de splen-do - re; de te, al -

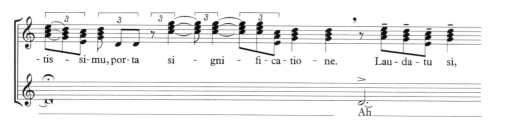

- tis - si - mu, por - ta si - gni - fi - ca - tio - ne. Lau - da - tu si,

Ah___

mi si - gno - re,   per so - ra lu - na___ e le stel - le;___ in ce - lu

Ah___

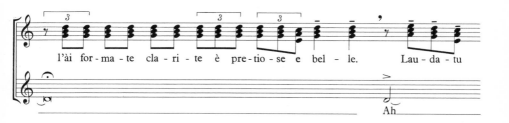

l'ài for - ma - te cla - ri - te è pre - tio - se e bel - le.   Lau - da - tu

Ah___

si, mi si - gno - re, per fra - te ven - tu____ e per a - e -

Ah_____

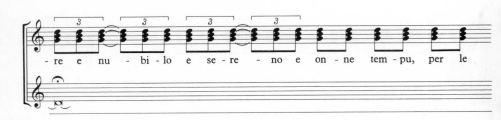

- re e nu - bi - lo e se - re - no e on - ne tem - pu, per le

qua - le a le tu - e cre - a - tu - re dà - i su - sten - ta - men - tu.

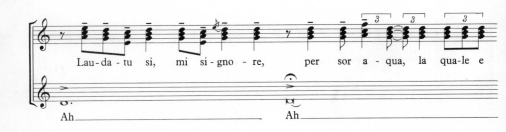

Lau - da - tu si, mi si - gno - re, per sor a - qua, la qua - le e

Ah_____ Ah_____

mul - to u - ti - le e hu - me - le e pre - tio - sa e ca - sta.

Ah_____

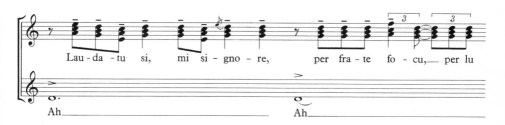

Lau - da - tu si,   mi si - gno - re,   per fra - te fo - cu,___ per lu

Ah_____   Ah_____

qua - le n'al - lu - me - ni   la noc - te; e el - lu è bel - lu   e io -

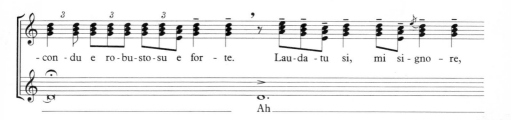

- con - du e ro - bu - sto - su e for - te.   Lau - da - tu si,   mi si - gno - re,

Ah_____

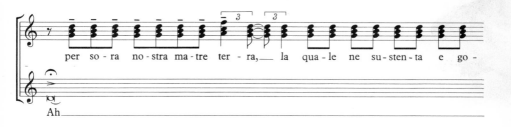

per so - ra no - stra ma - tre ter - ra,___ la qua - le ne su - sten - ta e go -

Ah_____

- ver - na e pro - du - ce   di - ver - si fru - cti e co - lo - ra - ti

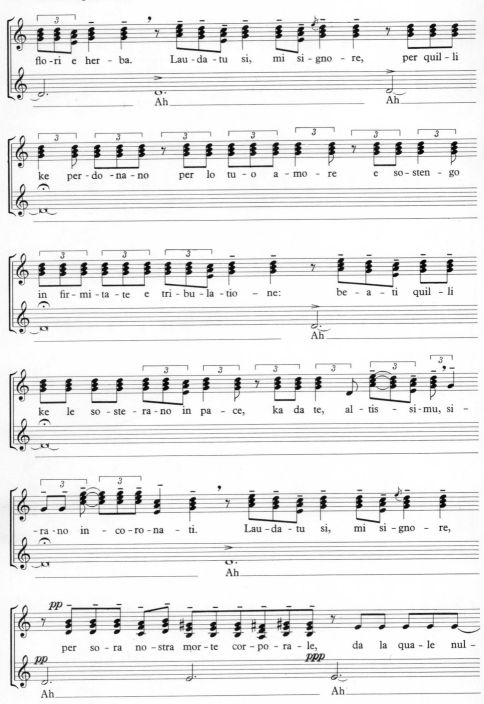

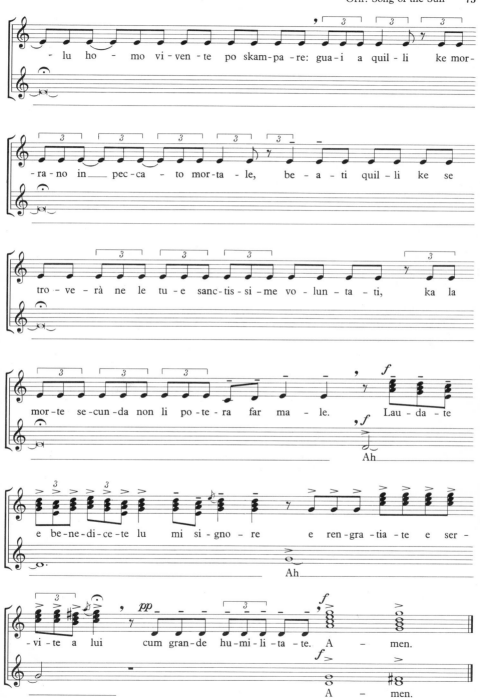

22. GOOD-NATURE TO ANIMALS

CHRISTOPHER SMART
(1722—1770)

PHYLLIS TATE

The words are from *Hymns for the Amusement of Children* by Christopher Smart.

3. What shall I whip in cru - el wrath The steed that bears me safe, Or 'gainst the dog, who plights his troth, For faith - ful ser - vice chafe. Which

4. In the deep wa - ters throw thy bread,

full,   Nor   let   neg - lect - ed   Dor - mice   sleep   To

full,   Nor   let   neg - lect - ed   Dor - mice   sleep   To

death   with-in   their   wool.   6. Tho'__   these   some   spi - rits

death   with-in   their   wool.   6. Tho'__   these   some   spi - rits

think   but   light,   And__   deem   in - dif - fer - ent   things;__

think   but   light,   And   deem   in - dif - fer - ent   things;

23. CHRIST THE LORD IS RISEN AGAIN

Words by MICHAEL WIESSE (c. 1480–1534)
tr. Catherine Winkworth
(1829–1878)

JOHN RUTTER

Note: Organ registration should be kept bright and clear.
Also published for mixed voices, S.A.T.B. (E124)

Ⓒ Oxford University Press 1973

151
1st and 2nd SOPRANOS
f
ALTOS
Al - le - lu - ia, al - le - lu - ia, al - le - lu-ia, al -
f
Al - le - lu - ia, al - le - lu - ia, al - le - lu-ia, al -
151
Ch. or Gt.
f
Ped.
157
- le - lu - ia!
Sw. mf
Gt. f
Man.
162
S. f
A.
5. Thou, our Pas - chal Lamb in - deed,
Sw.
Ped.
168
Christ, to - day thy peo - ple
Gt.

24. ANTHEM FOR THE TRINITY

(Suitable from Trinity Sunday until Advent)

ROBERT SHERLAW JOHNSON

★ Only essential features of registration and general level of dynamics are indicated in the organ part. The organist should feel free to use the full potential of his instrument along the lines indicated.

† The tone-quality required from the voices should be firm, and as 'reedy' as possible, without any trace of breathiness.

Printed in Great Britain

Lord___ have mer - cy___ on   us.

Sanc -tus im-mor -ta - lis   mi -se -re -re   no - bis.___

Sanc - tus,   sanc - tus,

Sanc - tus,   sanc - tus,   sanc -

Sanc - tus,   sanc - tus,   sanc -

★The organ doubling of the voice part may be omitted here.

Appendix